# The Tacky Manager

John E. Halbert

Illustrated by Karl R. Merriman

Published in Nashville, Tennessee, by ISI Publishing,
a division of Impact Seminars, Inc. in Brentwood, Tennessee.

Printed in the United States of America
by Vaughn Printing, Nashville, Tennessee

Some names, events, and anecdotes have been fictionalized
for protection of privacy.

Library of Congress
Catalog Card Number 91-90601

Halbert, John E., 1942-
The Tacky Manager.

1. Personal development.  2. Management.  3. Self-help.

Printing: 987654321

ISBN 0-9630968-1-8

# THE TACKY MANAGER

### by John E. Halbert

For more than ten years John Halbert has collected tacky illustrations, stories, and quotes about how managers relate to their employees. John believes that through humor, employers **and** employees can address barriers which have been erected as a result of employers' tacky behavior. John understands that employees can be tacky too, but that is another book!

As a consultant and seminar presenter, John has heard almost every conceivable story that keeps employees from being more effective in their work. At the same time, employers are asking why they get negative responses from their employees. Reading *The Tacky Manager* might be the first step away from the "them vs. us" mentality and a step toward a positive employee/employer relationship.

### Illustrations by Karl R. Merriman

Karl Merriman is a free lance cartoonist from Clarksville, Tennessee. Karl recognizes tacky when he sees it, and he successfully captures it with his pen. It is easy to relate to Karl's characters when he draws expressions that we, unfortunately, have all seen before.

As you look at the illustrations, you might see glimpses of past managers, and you may even see yourself. If you do, in that moment between awareness and denial, smile; allow the humor to challenge your past behavior.

# DEDICATION

This book is dedicated to my past tacky managers, to the tacky managers described by participants in seminars across the country, and to all of us who in moments of stress, duress, and panic have acted like a tacky manager.

And to Mother who said, "If you can't say anything nice, don't say anything at all."

# ACKNOWLEDGEMENTS

Thanks to Al Shackleford, Floyd and Anne Craig, and Christy Halbert for editing suggestions. To David Lill, Kathryn Collins, and Doug Jones for their continuing encouragement. To Keri Halbert for making it necessary that this book be commercially successful. To Margie Halbert for continuing to believe in the possibilities.

And to Tim Fields of Fields Communications and Publishing for additional help in editing, for typesetting, graphic design, and for taking a personal interest in *The Tacky Manager*.

# INTRODUCTION

If you found this book on your desk, do not look for the owner. It is yours! Someone who sees potential for your personal growth and development has given you *The Tacky Manager*, hopefully, in the spirit in which it was written... a humorous way to look at situations where managers can improve relationships with their employees.

If enough tacky managers read this book, it could make a significant difference in closing the gap between the U.S. and our off-shore competition. It could give your organization an edge in recruiting. And it could even help eradicate theft and sabotage on the part of angry employees.

How can a book about tacky managers do all of that? In most organizations there are employees who do not always perform as mature professionals. They are *not* looking for ways to make a significant contribution toward the mission of the organization. If you were to conduct an informal survey of these employees, you would find that often their justification for poor behavior correlates directly to the relationship with their immediate supervisors.

Just ask employees who are continually in trouble with management why they are non-performers. Ask them why they pull immature stunts and generally give their supervisors a hard time. I think you will find that they will justify their actions by talking about the *ineffectiveness* of their supervisors, their tacky managers.

Before we can get serious about quality improvement, we will have to get serious about rooting out tacky behavior on the part of management. Before we can deal with self-directed work teams or empowerment of associates, managers must recognize the high cost of tacky behavior and become effective leaders.

# TABLE OF CONTENTS

## PART II

And another thing. Until your attitude improves, you'll never get ahead around here. If you didn't whine about raises and benefits, maybe you might get more money. You never hear **me** whine about more money. You don't have an appreciation for all the work *I* do!

# WHAT IS TACKY?

"Tacky", as used in this book, is the practice of relating to employees as lessor beings. It is degrading and embarrassing. It belittles. It emphasizes differences in grades or classification of employees and management. It often attacks people where they are most vulnerable.

Tacky is unnecessary. It is not part of a healthy work environment. It destroys effective communication and trust. Tacky, as you will see in the true tacky anecdotes, is often against policies, procedures, regulations, good business practices, and the law! And, unfortunately it may be the only way some managers know how to relate!

# IS THERE HUMOR IN TACKY?

Tacky is so absurd, so inappropriate, so destructive to good business and to the improvement of quality of products and services, that some employees who have experienced a tacky manager ... quit. Some quit and leave, some quit and stay on the payroll, and others just laugh! They are able to find humor in the absurd, and continue to survive (i.e. keep their jobs), in spite of their hostile environments. Unfortunately, they begin playing not to lose, rather than playing to excel.

> "Humor allows us to distance ourselves from behavior. From a distance we can more clearly examine and understand behavior. Through understanding, the odds are greater that we can change or improve *our* behavior."
>
> Doug Jones

# ARE THE ANECDOTES TRUE?

Every example in *The Tacky Manager* is an employee's true story. They happened as they were written. In some instances the places have been changed to protect the employees' jobs.

While many successful organizations today refer to employees as **associates**, tacky managers refer to employees as "The girls, hey you, chief, *my* right hand man, *my* crew, or subordinates," just to name a few of their favorite labels.

A manager in a sales organization in New Brunswick marched into a support office and announced to the staff, "We are really backed up and I am down here to scrape the bottom of the barrel."

## WHAT IS THE TACKY MANAGER'S REACTION TO CONFRONTATION?

When tacky managers are confronted about the grief they are causing their employees, their response is, "I didn't realize that I was being tacky," or "I was misunderstood."

Other typical responses include:

"Subordinates are just too sensitive."

"I didn't mean anything by what I said."

"They are just too soft."

Something about a "hot kitchen."

"If they only realized how difficult my job is."

"Obviously, they were coddled."

"That was how I was taught."

"If my subordinates were more mature,
I would treat them differently."

"Tacky?  I'll show you tacky!"

How can managers treat employees with *less than* dignity and respect and then expect employees to treat customers or clients *with* dignity and respect?

## WHAT IS THE TACKY MANAGER'S ATTITUDE TOWARD EMPLOYEES?

Tacky managers make negative assumptions about people who report to them. These managers expect poor behavior from employees and seem to be disappointed when proven wrong. They would say to forget empowerment when you have a work force that does not have *integrity, objectivity, or competence.* "You just can't hire good people anymore." This *self-fulfilling prophecy* not only deters growth, it enhances turnover.

Tacky managers want things done right! They define right as how **they** would do it. They want their employees to fill in the blank with the one word they are thinking, and any other option is *wrong*. They tend to hire people who think like they do. If an employee disagrees with his/her manager, it is an obvious signal for the manager to start looking for a replacement.

**For example:** An experienced educator in Arkansas has a manager who continually looks at his watch during conferences. The professor feels his manager is trying to intimidate him by indicating that *his* valuable time is being wasted. His body language is stating, **"You** are not very important."

## THE TACKY MANAGER ON VISION

While an effective leader fosters genuinely shared visions with their associates, the vision of the tacky manager is limited to *today*. An effective leader knows that creating a vision for an organization is a process that helps associates become a part of something larger than themselves. The

process of identifying the vision itself generates commitment. An effective leader approaches everyday issues and problems with the vision in mind. For the tacky manager's complete expose' on vision, turn to page 54.

## THE TACKY MANAGER ON TEAMWORK

While the tacky manager encourages competition among employees, successful organizations have learned that employees willing to share talents, and pool skills can solve difficult problems and discover effective solutions. The effective leader realizes how vital teamwork is for the learning, growing, changing, relevant, and competitive organization. The tacky manager's approach to effective teamwork and its value is found on page 54.

## THE TACKY MANAGER ON COMMUNICATION

The effective manager will spend 80 percent of his/her time listening. Tacky managers practice *one way* communication.

**The tacky manager's choice phrases include:**

"Listen to what I say."

"If I want your opinion, I'll ask for it."

"I am not going to say it but once."

"It is apparent what I want."

"I don't have time to listen."

"If I listen to you, I'll not get my work done."

"Just figure it out."

## THE TACKY MANAGER ON EMPOWERMENT

The effective leader creates an environment that supports employees' creativity, drive toward excellence, competency, and responsibility.  The tacky manager says, "You can't let the prisoners run the prison."

## REAL LIFE ANECDOTES

Instead of being direct and describing the desired behavior change, a manager in Minneapolis used a tacky phrase and lost any hope of open dialogue that could result in the employee's improved performance.  The employee, working two jobs at minimum wage, was told by her night job manager, "Don't quit your day job"!

A business in Miami that requires employees to frequently work overtime (an indication of poor planning), provides the evening meal for employees and gives them a choice of hamburgers or pizza.  Instead of asking employees to "Please work late" or "Would you mind working late?" or "We really need help tonight" or any number of combinations which indicates some degree of respect to the employee, the manager struts in and asks, "What do you want to eat tonight?"

When someone is needed to help move tables or help with some other task requiring only a strong back, a manager in a Management Information Systems shop in Philadelphia says, "I need your expertise on this."

When clerical support personnel in a government office in Baltimore were told that they needed to give up their offices to make room for the *professionals* who needed the space, they were disappointed, but worked through it pretty well. They were cramped, disturbed by the lack of privacy, and had difficulty concentrating on their work, but were making a remarkable adjustment, until a manager waltzed in and said, "How are you girls doing down here in the pit?"

A seasoned employee in a manufacturing company near Louisville carefully explained that it was impossible to complete the current assignments, leave on time to meet his family at his child's school play, and take on a last minute *somewhat important* task. His manager listened, turned, and while walking off said, "Fit it in!"

There is a manager in Atlanta who begins every request with "I know you won't want to do this, I sure don't." If an employee complains about the *dirty work*, the manager's rebuttal is "That is why I hired you!"

In Mobile, a timid, but hard-working construction worker was the only employee willing to confront his foreman about an unsafe practice. Missing an opportunity to praise the worker for looking out for the interest of the company, his manager angrily retorted, "If you can't hack it, get your jacket!"

In a non-government but *very* bureaucratic organization in Washington D.C., a contract specialist brought a lamp from her home to use in her office. When her manager told her, "Your grade does not merit a lamp," she removed the lamp and promptly got a note from her doctor stating that she got headaches from fluorescent lights and she needed the incandescent lamp for health reasons. When asked if she brought the lamp back to the office, she stated, "I brought two!"

In the same agency, another employee was given the only office available at the time the employee was hired. The office was one foot too wide for her grade. During the next year, prior to her leaving the agency, at least once a week her manager reminded her, "Your office is too big for you!"

A service business in St. Louis has a manager known for creating fear and mistrust by slipping around and surprising employees with terse statements like, "What are you doing and why are you doing it?"

A flight attendant, at 35,000 feet, said her manager could never give her a compliment without adding some negative comment. On one occasion while being debriefed after a training flight, she heard, "You were perfect in every area, but you do have little fuzzballs on your apron." Tacky managers have not learned to give praise without adding a "**but.**"

A Rhode Island sales clerk was told by her manager to use her best judgement and do whatever it takes to appease their customers. When her manager was away, an irate customer began making a scene demanding that his money be returned for clothing his daughter did not like. Other customers were beginning to show signs of feeling uncomfortable and in the hope of future business with the customer, the clerk smiled and accommodated the customer. When her manager returned and learned what happened, she announced in a loud voice, "You once again showed poor judgement. You did not handle the situation the way I would have!" You can easily spot the store in the mall. It is the one with the permanent *help wanted* sign in the window.

A woman in the Midwest was running a one person office and reported directly to the owner. On one particular occasion, she took the initiative and made a phone call to gather information for the owner to make an educated decision. She was raked over the coals with "Who do you think you are? Do you think this is your business?" Even some tacky managers would see the value of having an associate who treats the business with a sense of ownership.

In a company of about eighty employees, the President and his wife give the female employees a small gift at Christmas, not the men. While it is intended to be a thoughtful expression of appreciation, it is perceived by a majority of the women as a tacky statement: You are not considered as professionals and we pay you less so we'll give you a little gift.

When hired as an agency accountant and told her new title was Accounting Division Manager, a woman in Ohio assumed she had an important role in the agency. In the recruiting process, she had even been told her new position was an essential management position. At the next Annual Meeting, all of the management group were introduced, but she was overlooked by the Executive Director. When the oversight was brought to the attention of the Executive Director, she responded as a tacky manager with "She is just our accountant."

Often when tacky managers are challenged on an unreasonable or non-defendable directive and cannot quickly determine the appropriate tacky response, they fall back on the old reliable phrase "Because I'm the boss, that's why!"

---

### FAMOUS TACKY MANAGER ONE LINERS:

"Because that's the way it is and if you don't like it, you can leave."

"If my initials are on the memo, you do it."

"That's your problem."

"It says right here, other duties as assigned."

"You'll get your raise when I get mine."

"So?"

"Your job is to make me look good."

"You're elected."

"Just do it!"

---

At the end of a computer sales meeting to *motivate* the sales force, the manager's closing comment was "Everyone who makes his sales forecast gets to keep his job."

Sometimes managers get close to saying something positive, but they often *blow it* at the last minute. Like the manager who said, "I want to tell you it has been a lot easier working with you today."

Forget training when the managers' approach to professional growth and development is, "I don't send these people to seminars. We're paying for their time, not their brains."

Employees in a financial services office were asked about their manager's tacky behavior and two of the favorite responses were:

(1) their manager leaves early when there are major system problems and does not even inquire about the problems the following day.

(2) their manager says there will be major changes in their careers but then waits two days before information is disclosed.

When an employee asked to attend a personal growth and development seminar, the response was "You can't follow directions, you need to go to the follow directions seminar."

During a discussion with my *boss* about the quantity of assignments I had been given and the impossible time frame I was told to have them completed, I asked if it were quantity or quality he was most interested in. My manager replied, "I want quantity and quality, and if you can't give it to me, perhaps I should look for someone who can."

A banker in Atlanta just loves it when the managers he works with all day long will not speak to him on the elevator. "When I say hello, I am ignored."

Of course, at 5:00 on Friday tacky managers seem to have time for long casual conversations, if *they* are not in a hurry.

There are four people in our department, one manager and
three workers. The phones will be ringing off the hook and
we (the three workers) are with customers and we each
have calls on hold. Our manager refuses to pick up a line,
but he interrupts us to discuss an error made during this
busy time.

## SOME FUN TACKY MANAGER
## ONE OR TWO LINERS

"There is no ball and chain on your foot. If you don't
like what you are doing - get out!"

"No, you can't take your vacation next month
because of the project and besides I will be on
vacation."

"You are history."

"This is war. It is your job or mine. You lose."

"Can't you people get anything done?"

"Since you're not doing anything ..."

"I don't care if you want to do it, just do it! And
don't #*@$*! it up this time."

"What kind of an increase/bonus do you want - candy
or gum?"

"In this company we are a democracy. Everyone has
a vote, but only my vote counts."

"When is it due? This time yesterday."

"I don't have time, I'm management."

## TACKY MANAGERS EVEN PUT IT IN WRITING!

Internal memo regarding clean-up: "I have asked you politely and now I am telling you very emphatically - there is to be no, I repeat no eating in the classroom (especially the typing and computer labs). Our school quickly deteriorates unless we constantly monitor the cleanliness. We have to live here a long time, folks, please do your part. Please announce to your students that the vending machines will be turned off for one week unless people can learn how to clean up after themselves."

A memo in the Billing Department of an electrical parts company: "You are too busy for the project. Have one of the girls do it."

And speaking of building a positive relationship with women in the office, at his retirement party, a V.P. over sales and a certified tacky manager, announced to his replacement who would be supervising three women, "I'm leaving these lovely things to you."

## THE TACKY MANAGER IS NOT BOUND BY THE TRUTH

We had several meetings on what employees want from the director. One year later, we had a meeting to hear a response.

"Your job will be restructured." Several months later I am still wondering when.

"I don't care what we agreed to in the beginning of the year. That's too much money to pay you as a bonus."

We've been trying to get new forms ready for two years. My manager keeps telling me every two or three weeks, "I know I have to get with you on those forms, but I don't have any time for you right now."

## WHAT REALLY IRRITATES EMPLOYEES

When seminar participants were asked what their managers had done that *really* bothered them, they made the following contributions.

My manager said, "I am not at liberty to tell you yet, but major changes are in the works. I can't tell you about them."

Being told to get it done during lunch and everyone else goes to lunch.

Sign on the wall in the manager's office, "You can't be fired - you can't fire slaves."

"It's tough luck you got pregnant."

After a woman got promoted, my manager's comment was, "See, women get ahead by sleeping around."

Making unnecessary personal remarks about me when I am not around - not addressing me directly.

Starting his conversations with, "And, as I was saying ..."

Verbally abusing personnel in front of others.

After saying, "We'll all do this together," my manager leaves.

"I got this request three weeks ago, I need this back in twenty minutes."

She just doesn't listen, ever.

Ignoring a potential problem until it becomes a problem; then *forgetting* that it was previously brought to her attention.

Tapping on the desk while I am trying to talk.

Patronizing. Sometimes this happens when I *think* my manager is trying to help.

After complaining about something I did on the job, my manager took over the project and left me out.

"You need to get this done!"

From 1:00 to 4:30 - I'm not busy.
4:45 - I hear, "This will only take twenty minutes."
7:00 - I'm still working on it.

In an exit interview I learned that a manager in my company had said, "When I ask, speak. Until then, shut up and sit down."

"If in fact you are sick on a certain day, please let me know a few days in advance."

Taking credit for my ideas and jobs I have done.

## MORE STORIES FROM THE TRENCHES

A customer called wanting a special price and I asked my manager for guidance. He gave me the price and after I called the customer and stated the price and delivery date and said that this was the best we could do, my manager changed his mind and had me call the customer with our *new and improved lower price.*

My manager has a habit of promising things and *never* following through.

My manager will delegate authority and then not stand behind me.

A woman wanted an application for employment. We had never hired a woman for the factory because of the lifting requirements and I mentioned that fact to the applicant. Before I could explain the reasons, my manager started yelling at me, "You can't do that. Are you trying to get us sued?" He continued in front of the woman until I closed the window and asked my manager to please not berate me in front of people. I opened the window, apologized to the woman, and gave her an application. I wish he would hear the whole story before blowing up.

I was given a promotion by a vice-president (my tacky manager), and two weeks later, he told me the promotion wasn't quite as all he had told me it was—a different title, smaller office, and the same responsibilities as my *old job*.

My manager tells me to tell a customer "No, No, No!" Then when the customer demands to see my manager, he says, "Oh, just tell them yes."

> My manager just can't resist the *I'm better than you mentality*. Like: "Sweetie, take care of the coffee pot."

My position required that I dress at work in a three piece suit and because I did not comply, a dress code policy was issued for all employees. This was a new job and I did not have the money for a new wardrobe. My manager never talked to me directly about my behavior.

Five minutes before a presentation to a group of bankers my manager said, "If you don't do well, I will embarrass you while you're presenting your work."

On a job interview, I asked my manager to describe his management style. He said with a slight grin, "I like to give people enough rope to hang themselves." I thought he was kidding!

While helping another division when the workload was extremely heavy, a manager said, "You don't count; you're not one of ours."

"If it were easy, we would have women doing it."

When I proposed a new idea, my manager replied, "I'm too busy right now. I'll talk to you later." She was making a grocery list!

"With all the work you have to do, you have time to laugh?"

"I would like to have **this** work done on time."

"Okie dokie, this is the way we are going to do it. I don't care what the input is, okie dokie?"

"I'd like to run my fingers through your hair."

"More men should get hired because they don't get pregnant."

"I don't know if I can afford to keep you or not."

A situation happened while I was on vacation that I had no control over. My manager said, "While you were on vacation, my business was going down the tubes."

"Here. Do This. No hurry, it doesn't matter anyway."

"I know you probably will do this wrong, but i'm going to give you a chance anyway."

## And Tacky Managers Wonder
## Why Subordinates Avoid Them...

"I know Joe is incapable, but let him do it anyway. We can clean it up later."

"We can take care of this tomorrow, that is if you are here."

If you ask my manager too many questions, his response is, "Just put it down - I'll do it later."

In the course of discussing a problem in my area of responsibility, my manager said, "You should be at home, barefoot and pregnant."

---

**Have you noticed how many of the examples are not only tacky, but are illegal?**

---

My manager, who had let several letters sit on her desk for two days, said, "Don't keep putting the wrong dates on these letters."

"I can't understand why it can't be done my way."

In response to a technical question my manager said, "What am I, your college professor?"

Six months ago my plane was late coming back from vacation and I was tardy for work. Recently, after surgery I needed a second day off with my doctor's suggestion, my manager's response was, "I'm feeling abused by your needs."

"If you do a good job, you won't get a raise. You will get to keep your job."

"You can be transferred!"

"Management is not getting paid this week since we have to pay you guys."

"Where will you be working tomorrow?"

"I will fight you tooth and nail on this."

On more than one occasion, my manager has said he needs to speak with me about something and then he will pause and say, "Oh, maybe not now." I am not sure how I need to handle this. All it does is make me paranoid that I've done something wrong.

My manager's new employee orientation included this statement, "If you steal from me, you will go to jail! I won't feel sorry for you."

Every situation in which someone can be involved, my manager has experienced it and has always handled it better than the eleven people he supervises.

When I asked my manager to help me decide about changing careers, she said, "I don't want to play this game. Make a decision."

"This really shouldn't be part of your job, but I want you to do it anyway."

"You work for the company, don't you? Well, then you should be willing to be more flexible with your time, even your personal time. You owe it to us. Don't you like your job?"

"If you want to be transferred, this is the time to do it because there are going to be some changes around here."

I went into my manager's office to get keys out of her desk. She did not let me know that it bothered her, but told several employees that it did. I confronted her and she brought up several things that happened six months ago, but she never mentioned them to me at the time.

"Let that sink in!"

"Every positive outcome is to my credit. It is a good thing the company has me."

"You're not even doing the basics. I can't tell you how to do it. You'll have to figure it out yourself."

"We are paying you all this money to do the job. You should not complain about the job. If you don't like doing the job, you should leave the agency."

I worked at a psychiatric hospital as a social worker with nurses, doctors, secretaries, and other professionals. When I offered an opinion my manager said, "But, you are only a social worker."

"Are you sure you can get this done? Your team always seems to be behind."

On the evaluation form for the 180 day probation period my manager added, "Please initial if employee **does not** meet our standards. If you want to retain the employee, please explain why."

My manager threw a document down on my desk which I had edited and said, "I can't believe you'd miss that mistake!" She said it loud enough for everyone to hear.

At a time when salary adjustments were being made, I asked my manager how she determined who got what. She said, "I give them what I want to give them."

At 4:55 p.m. - "This contract has to go in the mail tonight." It had not even been typed yet.

When I told my manager that a client was unhappy with our company he said, "The client has a problem."

I was told by my manager, when working late one evening trying to meet a deadline, "Why are you here? All this overtime isn't impressing anyone." I was not even claiming overtime, but did afterwards.

"Since you are going on vacation tomorrow, you can stay late tonight."

I sold a service directly to customers, but the service turned out to be far different than what I had represented. My manager's defense was, "Promise them everything, give them nothing."

I met with my supervisor and another manager to discuss my situation regarding travel. I explained that I didn't want to travel on the weekends because my husband was gone all week. My supervisor said I would have to make a decision. I told him I wouldn't get a divorce over my job and he said, "I will support you if you get a divorce."

I was looking over the staff and employee birthday list and noticed that the person whose place I took had the exact same birthday. I commented on this to my manager and he said, "Darn, I sure hope you're nothing like she was. We had to fire her for poor job performance."

My manager told me to make decisions at my own discretion. When I told her about a situation and what I did, she said, "You should have never done that without consulting me first."

"If you don't like the way things are done around here I suggest you talk to the president of the company!"

During a performance evaluation, my manager told me, "Well, you don't have any big problems, but everyone can find something to improve on."

After applying for a promotion that I did not get, my manager called me into her office and told me, "Really, there weren't any candidates that were qualified."

"Fix this!" was written in large letters and circled on my memo with no explanation.

When confused about a procedure used for starting an account in the computer, I asked how to handle the situation. My manager responded in front of others, "I can't believe you don't know how to do that. We talked about it in your job interview."

An employee who looks happy is not acting like a professional!

As a new supervisor in a personnel department, I was really surprised when my manager's secretary asked to talk with me about her unhappiness with her work. I spent several hours over a few weeks listening. I then suggested that her options *included* working somewhere else. I learned later, my manager, had sent her to see me with a *fake* problem and my manager began telling people that I was ***encouraging*** employees to leave.

I turned in a request for vacation time, and the following day my manager left a note requesting, "This time be truthful." The whole incident happened because I did not tell her why I wanted my vacation at that particular time. We had a terrible argument after she called me a *liar.*

My manager had been with the company for twelve years and decided to leave. I had been offered her position so I asked for any advice she had and any other tips regarding supervising. After six weeks, she still refuses to offer any advice, will barely speak to me, and when she does, is very hostile.

My manager demanded that I hire someone who was not qualified and explained it by saying, "Life isn't fair. Some people get hired because of who they know."

I was on jury duty. Another employee was with me. She was sent home, but I was not. The third morning I received a call from my manager, "You know, if you are not supposed to report for jury duty, you are supposed to report to work."

When talking with employees about very unpopular rule changes, my manager made the statement, "I don't make the rules - I enforce them. If you don't like it, the door swings both ways."

I corrected an error on work which my manager handed in and informed her. She responded, "In the highly unlikely event that you are correct ..."

"Here, sign this. This is your evaluation. We don't have time to go over it now. This is what your raise is. Sign it and next year you will get a 10 percent increase." All of this was said in front of others and nine months later we still have not discussed it.

"That is not your problem. Don't worry about it."

"So what do you want me to do about it?"

A co-worker wanted recognition for her work and her manager said, "Apparently you don't know what it means to be a team player. I had this problem with another woman, too. Here's how it works, you work for me and when you make me look good, you'll get ahead."

My manager told me, "I want to see you before you leave." It was 3:05 and I leave at 3:30. He then proceeded to get involved with someone else until 3:25. He gave me a raise, but it was still tacky.

"I wouldn't give this to you, but my manager is making me."

"I don't know why they hired a woman for this position."

"We are about to lose our funding, and it is all your fault!"

I called my manager for a direct answer to a staff shortage problem and a variety of other problems that needed solutions and his approval. He offered no help, but responded with, "Welcome to management."

My manager only criticizes people when they are out of the room.

My manager asked me for a report and when I told him I wanted to get some ideas from my team, he said, "You are not coming across as a strong manager if you talk with your subordinates about what they think."

My manager thinks he is cute when he says, "What are you doing out of your cubby?"

I was working at my desk, drinking a soft drink, when my manager stuck her head in the door and said, "Are you enjoying your Sprite?" Two days later, same situation, my manager asked, "Is that my Sprite?" When I told her that I bought it, she said, "It must be the cleaning staff stealing my Sprites."

\*\*\*

*This collection of tacky anecdotes was contributed by employees and managers in forty-six states. While some of the tacky managers' comments are unethical, all of them are costly to organizations!*

# The Tacky Manager

# Part II

# PART II

Part II of *The Tacky Manager* addresses the skills and techniques necessary to become a tacky manager, like:

- Running meetings,

- Making effective use of time,

- Handling the telephone,

- Making the 15 Points work for you,

- Recognizing tacky choices,

- Dealing with subordinates' problems, and

How to deal with your current situation, featuring...

- How to **help** *your* tacky manager,

- How to **tell** if **you** are a tacky manager,

- What to **do** if you **are** a tacky manager,

- What to **do** if you **have** a tacky manager, and

- The **Official Tacky Manager Test.**

Plus

- An opportunity for you to order some *tacky stuff*,

- A request for your *tacky stories*.

- Suggested Resources, and information

- About the Author

## HOW DOES A TACKY MANAGER RUN A MEETING?

When meetings *must* be held (a tacky manager will do almost anything to keep from having a meeting), the following guidelines are followed by the *Tacky Manager*.

1.  Announce the meeting when you are ready to meet. If you give your subordinates a warning they might ask for an agenda.

2.  Never have an agenda. Surprising your subordinates will keep you in control.

3.  Arrive late to indicate that you are more important than your subordinates.

4.  Keep the sun at your back, give them short chairs, and keep the meeting room too cool or too warm. If you keep them uncomfortable they won't ask for so many meetings.

5.  Put your personal awards, diplomas, certificates, and a large picture of a lion eating a lamb on the wall.

6.  At the last minute ask one of the *girls* to take notes.

7.  After the meeting throw away the notes.

8.  Ask a subordinate for a report that you know is not ready. The reaction of the individual and of the group will again elevate your position.

9.  Do not announce a stop time. When you are tired of the meeting - adjourn.

10. Have your secretary call during meetings. Take the "calls" and pretend to carry on a conversation. This strategy will add to your importance.

11. If a subordinate wants to modify your agenda, quickly remind the group whose meeting it is.

12. Don't let anyone talk you into evaluating your meetings' effectiveness or efficiency. It will just turn into a personal attack and you don't need to discuss anything that will not change.

13. If you are not careful, *they* will start to use meetings for routine planning and for reporting on what happens between meetings. Keep talking. When asking questions, ask for their response by a *show of hands*.

# THE TACKY MANAGER'S IDEAS
# ON EFFECTIVE TIME MANAGEMENT
## A QUICK REFERENCE GUIDE

1. Your subordinate's time is *your* time. There is no such thing as interrupting an employee.

2. Recognizing and defining time wasters *is* a waste of time.

3. The illusion of busyness is more important than the effectiveness of planning.

4. Read newspapers and magazines at work because you are thinking about work when you are at home.

5. Feel guilty about what you do not do, and feeling guilty will let you off the hook.

6. When you have tough decisions - procrastinate. There are few things so important you can not put them off.

7. Have confidence in your own judgment of priorities regardless of what evidence your subordinates present.

8. Always work alone on creative projects so you can take full credit.

9. Use a secretary for dictation rather than compose on your own computer and no one will accuse you of doing stuff (i.e., typing) that is beneath you.

10. When you become bored, drop in on your subordinates.

11. When you delegate, do not tell the delegatee everything you know and you will not sense a loss of control.

12. When in doubt about your best use of time - retreat to old attitudes, belief systems, and viewpoints.

13. A daily *do list* is for your subordinates;  you do not need to commit to how you plan to spend *your* day.

14. Put everything in writing to cover your "rear end."  Or, put nothing in writing to cover your "rear end."

15. To prevent mistakes - whatever is presented to you - the best management strategy is to delay.

16. If you want anything done right, you had better do it yourself.

## THE TACKY MANAGER'S TELEPHONE HABITS*

### A TEST

Directions:  Check the tacky manager's telephone habits that **you** practice.

☐ 1.  My associates do not know where I am or when I plan to return when I am away from the phone - this prevents unrealistic expectations on the part of clients.

☐ 2.  I insist someone answers my phone to indicate to my clients that I am important and it gives my associates something to do.  Waiting for more than two rings (sometimes many more), I am saying that we are a **busy business** and you are lucky to reach us.

☐ 3.  I never give my name when calling and when I answer the phone I save time by not identifying myself.

☐ 4.  By not speaking clearly, naturally or pleasantly I am able to reduce the time taken on the phone with most clients.  Again, if I sound like I am too busy for them and that **I have been interrupted**, they will not keep me long on the phone.  Maybe, they will think twice before interrupting me in the future.

☐ 5.  I do not personalize conversations by using the caller's name.  It is obvious he/she knows who he/she is.

☐ 6.  I don't do messages!  If it is important, they will call back.

☐ 7.  I do not offer my help to a caller because to do so would just invite more questions.

☐ 8.  If pressed, I will take the caller's name and
     number, but I encourage the caller to **just call back**.

☐ 9.  If a caller has to wait more than a few minutes
     while they are on hold, they obviously don't mind.  If
     they did they are smart enough to hang up and call
     back later.

☐ 10. I use a speaker phone so I can do other things while I
     am talking to clients.

☐ 11. I don't bother to return calls - if it is really important
     *they* will call back.

☐ 12. Frequently, messages are just not important and
     should be delayed or never returned.

☐ 13. My secretary places my calls so I can do important
     things.

Scoring:    0 - You have **effective** telephone habits.

          1 to 4 - There is hope.

          5 to 11 - Write letters.  Stay away from the phone.

          12 or 13 - Hopefully, you misunderstood the directions.

* The telephone habits were *adapted* with permission of
Craig Communications Inc.

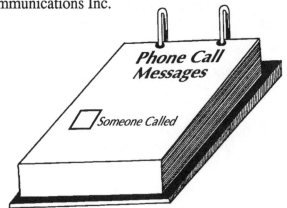

## THE FIFTEEN POINTS OF THE TACKY MANAGER

1.  Subordinates do not need to know or understand the purpose of *your business*. It is important to frequently remind them about whose business it is.

2.  Management is saddled with the responsibility for decisions. You didn't get this position by not being smart. You will need to hire others for extra hands to get *your work* done, but remember they do not care about anything, but the money.

3.  Inspection means it will not go out until it is *right*. If you have enough inspectors, you can catch employees messing up, punish them, and then ship products that are *good enough*. Sending extra products will insure that your clients will get enough of the good ones.

4.  Continue to look for vendors willing to bid on materials and then take the lowest bid. Treating vendors like expendable suppliers will keep them sharp and you will save money. Don't let *vendors* take over your company.

5.  If it's not broken, don't fix it. If there were better ways of doing things, you would be doing them. If things get tight, you can always save money by laying people off.

6.  Throw new employees into their work immediately. The better ones will figure it out. Orientation for employees who will not stay long is a waste of money.

7.  Institute *tight* control through the use of power and intimidation.

8.  Use fear as a motivator. People who are afraid of losing their jobs will pay careful attention and not make mistakes. Managers can do the innovating.

9. Keep departments separate. Institute competition between departments for your limited resources. Only management needs to have the *big picture*.

10. Use slogans, exhortations, and post on the wall goals of zero defects. Employees have to be **reminded** frequently about not hurting themselves and about not abusing the company. Don't spend time on training and development.

11. Establish production quotas for the factory floor as well as for marketing. Use management by numbers and numerical goals to control your subordinates. Remember: *Where there is a whip, there is a way.*

12. Maintain control with annual reviews. Remind them that *their review is coming!* Stress numbers rather than system improvement and emphasize *it only has to be good enough.*

13. Education is an expense. Certainly, any self-improvement training is not the organization's concern.

14. If something *must* change, it is the responsibility of managers who are the thinkers, not your subordinates who are the doers.

15. If you are ever tempted to allow your subordinates to participate in decision making - ask yourself this question, "If *they* are so smart, why aren't they the boss"?

*******

What does *The Tacky Manager* think about
TOTAL QUALITY CONTROL?

"IT IS GREAT! JUST LEAVE OUT
THE MIDDLE WORD."

# CHECK YOUR UNDERSTANDING

Select the column with the most *tacky* responses.

| A | B |
|---|---|
| Yeah, but | Let's try it |
| Keep working on it | It will work |
| Timing is not right | Wonderful |
| Maybe later | Excellent, very good |
| It's not your responsibility | How can I help |
| Slow down | Tell me more about it |
| Needs more research | Sounds like a great idea |
| It won't work | Really creative |
| Who told you to do it | Go for it |
| No | Yes |

**This one** ☐        **This one** ☐

Employees' reactions to column **A**:

1. Says: "This is the last time I'll offer an idea."
2. Blows up!
3. Walks away.
4. Gets quiet.

Employees' reactions to column **B**:

1. Says: "If you like that, I've got another idea that is even better."
2. Smiles!
3. Calls home and tells someone, "I'm appreciated!"
4. Increases participation.

## THE TACKY MANAGER'S APPROACH TO
## DEALING WITH SUBORDINATES' PROBLEMS

1. Down play subordinates' problems. Use distracting techniques like kidding or pushing problems aside to deal with something *really* important.

2. Sometimes shocking the subordinate with, "That's ridiculous," will snap them back to reality.

3. When you have heard enough - *solve* the problems for your subordinates - they would never figure it out on their own.

4. Lecturing and using logic to influence your employees with problems will assure their thinking twice about bringing it up again.

5. Just tell your subordinates what to do. They would not be telling you about a problem if they were not looking for you to solve the problem.

6. Short list of appropriate tacky manager responses:

    | | | |
    |---|---|---|
    | • **Moralizing** | • **Warning** | • **Advising** |
    | • **Ordering** | • **Admonishing** | • **Arguing** |
    | • **Commanding** | • **Directing** | • **Preaching** |
    | • **Threatening** | • **Instructing** | • **Criticizing** |

7. If subordinates have problems there must be something wrong with *them* and you need to fix them, so:

    • Ask a lot of questions.

    • Talk them out of their feelings.

    • Categorize, stereotype, and label.

    • Manipulate through flattery.

    • Judge/evaluate their actions.

8. If you try these suggestions and your subordinates continue to come back to you with their problems, try:

- **Blaming**
- **Name-calling**
- **Ridiculing**
- **Disagreeing**
- **Judging**
- **Shaming**

9. Remember, if you listen to *one* problem your subordinates will start lining up at your door and *expect* you to listen to theirs.

10. You are paid to **manage**, you are not paid to become their *nursemaid*!

It is obvious that you caused this problem—and I can't believe you did it!

# WHAT CAN YOU DO TO HELP YOUR TACKY MANAGER?

1. Don't ever *say* you are trying to help!

2. When you receive a rare compliment from your manager, simply reply with a "thank you." Overcome the temptation to argue, put yourself down, or offer a tacky response like "put it in my paycheck".

3. Show appreciation for your supervisor's strengths. Catch him/her doing it right. It **will** happen, if only by accident.

4. Keep your supervisor informed - no surprises.

5. Volunteer to do projects in which you have a special interest.

6. State your preference and don't expect your manager to read your mind.

7. Confront your manager at the time you are feeling attacked.

   When you hear a *tacky* barb, try this:

   > "When you said, _____ , I think I heard a barb in what you said. Did you mean it that way?" After hearing the denial or the barb again, state how you would prefer being treated. If it is difficult for you to be assertive you might state that it is difficult, but it is *that* important.

8. Don't say that you understand. You will have a better chance of being heard if you avoid *red flag words*. If your manager becomes defensive, try to find out what you said that is the *hook*.

9. You could try appealing to your manager's commitment to the organization's goals. Discuss the negative consequences of *tacky* behavior toward reaching those goals.

10. Find a mentor in the organization (one who is older and who has been with the organization a long time, and can keep a confidence), and ask for help.

## TELL-TALE INDICATORS
## OF
## THE TACKY MANAGER

How do you know if you are a tacky manager?

1.  After the holiday party at your house there is another one later - *everyone* is there - you hear about it several days later.

2.  People get real quiet when you walk into a room.

3.  No one disagrees with you.

4.  People tend to forget what you told them.

5.  You have received several copies of **THE TACKY MANAGER.**

6.  Turnover is high.

7.  You have told people that high turnover is good.

8.  Restroom walls are the primary source of communication.

9.  You are the *last* to find out what is going on.

10. Your family does not want to attend the open house at the office.

11. Production goes up when you are out of town.

12. You feel that if something happened to you the organization would fold.

## WHAT IF YOU ARE A TACKY MANAGER?

1. Join a *Tacky Manager* support group.

   WRITE:  TACKY MANAGER SUPPORT GROUP
   P.O. BOX 431
   BRENTWOOD, TN 37024-0431

2. Join a Federal Witness Protection Program.

3. Get a dog (you can be tacky to a dog and they will still do tricks).

## *or*

4. Begin a systematic reading program - **today!** Start with the Suggested Resources.

5. Listen to tapes, attend seminars and conferences. Again, start with the Suggested Resources.

6. Find a mentor.

7. Announce to your staff that they can expect to be treated differently.

8. Begin referring to your employees as your associates and start treating them as your associates.

9. Reread *The Tacky Manager* looking for the **effective leader's** response. Hint: The **effective leader's** response is opposite *The Tacky Manager's* approach.

10. Practice laughing at yourself. Do not take yourself so seriously that you miss the fun of leading an effective organization!

## WHAT DO YOU DO IF
## YOU HAVE A TACKY MANAGER?

1.  **Change jobs!**

### *or*

2.  **Practice creative confrontation:**

    • Ask for permission to bring up something that is difficult to discuss.

    • Is this an okay time for us to discuss something that may require change, but could allow me to become more productive? or

    • I am uncomfortable with something that is going on around us and if you would be willing to discuss it with me I think it could improve our productivity.

    • When you are in private, on neutral turf (or at least on your manager's turf), in the morning hours, and on a *good day*, begin with a description of specific examples.

    Yesterday, when you _____

    I felt _____ Because I _____

    Pause for discussion (avoid defensiveness)

    What I would like is _____

    Because _____

    **Ask: Am I on track?**

    Spend 80 percent of the discussion listening to your manager.

    Let the manager speak first. If you speak first, when you are talking your manager may be thinking about what to say when you inhale.

    Repeat what is said to check out if what you heard is what was intended.

    Add something that will substantiate your manager's position.

> Comment on the reasonableness of your manager's position.
>
> Indicate where you are in agreement.
>
> State your desired outcome and mention how you both will benefit.
>
> Ask for feedback on the manager's perception.
>
> Agree on action to be taken.
>
> Thank your manager for his/her investment in improving the situation.

**If #2 doesn't work, you don't have a chance**, but you might try the next suggestions before you go back to #1.

3. Purchase scores of *The Tacky Manager* and leave them in strategic places.

4. Just tell yourself it won't bother you. Decide that you can live with a tacky manager and that it will not affect your work. Of course, **it will**. Popular ways people cope with a tacky manager include:

   • **Overeating**    • **Using alcohol**    • **Using other drugs**

   • **Becoming ill**    • **Smoking**    • **Abusing someone**

5. Quit and stay on the payroll. Do just enough to get by and don't make waves. Request that everything be put in writing.

6. Look for opportunities to put your manager on the spot.

7. Revenge is so sweet and you'll not have to worry about writing a letter of resignation. Go around your manager and present your complaints to his/her manager. However, update your resume' before attempting this maneuver and seek legal counsel.

8. Start blaming co-workers for mistakes and problems to take the pressure off of you.

# THE OFFICIAL TACKY MANAGER TEST

Directions: Select **all** of the *Tacky Manager's* responses to the following scenarios.

1. An employee calls the office five minutes after the office opens and explains that when he left home this morning he was experiencing chest pains. As he began to drive the pains got worse and he is now in the emergency room at the local hospital. You say:

   ❑ A. Do you realize you have no sick leave?

   ❑ B. We'll hold your job until 11:00.

   ❑ C. You should call in before you are going to be late.

   ❑ D. Is there anything that we can do? Could we call someone? Don't worry about things here...

2. An employee is asked to retrieve a file and after looking for several minutes reports that it can't be found. You say:

   ❑ A. I hired you to keep things straight.

   ❑ B. Do you not know how to file?

   ❑ C. You must have lost it.

   ❑ D. I may have misfiled it. Have you tried...?

3. Later when the file is found on your desk, you say.

   ❑ A. I told you it was on my desk.

   ❑ B. You should have known I had it.

   ❑ C. Nothing.

   ❑ D. Thanks for looking, but I found it on my desk. Sorry for the wild goose chase.

4. An employee turns in a project that has been exceptionally well done. You say:

   ❏ A. Nothing.

   ❏ B. Why can't you do this kind of work all of the time?

   ❏ C. Nothing. *Then type a new cover page with your name on it.*

   ❏ D. This is an exceptionally well done project. Thank you for your extra efforts.

5. An employee does something against the company's written policy and procedures manual. You say:

   ❏ A. Are you trying to commit career suicide?

   ❏ B. This really doesn't surprise me.

   ❏ C. Well, at least I know what kind of an employee you are.

   ❏ D. This behavior is so unlike you, help me understand...

6. An employee without being asked has come up with a super idea. You say:

   ❏ A. Apparently you don't have enough to do.

   ❏ B. Are you deliberately trying to make me look bad?

   ❏ C. I had already thought of that years ago.

   ❏ D. Wow!

7. Your customer service group has been telling you for sometime that they are in need of additional representatives and now they are talking about a way to prevent so many complaints. Something about improvement of quality. You say:

    ❑ A. What goes on in other departments is none of your business.

    ❑ B. You've got to work faster and not goof off so much.

    ❑ C. If our quality gets too good, you are out of a job.

    ❑ D. You are right. In our staff meeting Tuesday we can explore ways to communicate the feedback we are getting to the rest of the company and how to get relief during peak periods.

8. A new employee asks to talk to you about a problem related to her lack of training on her job. You say:

    ❑ A. If you can't hack it, get your jacket.

    ❑ B. You misrepresented yourself to me. I thought you were smart enough to handle the job.

    ❑ C. Grow up! You are acting like a little child. Your problem is nothing.

    ❑ D. Do you have some ideas on how to get the assistance you need?

9. An employee misses *another* deadline. You say:

    ❑ A. Nothing. Just note it in the file.

    ❑ B. Are you trying to ruin my career?

    ❑ C. It looks like you have an attitude problem.

    ❑ D. Since this is becoming the norm, I would like to hear what you can do to improve the system to prevent delays.

10.   You have just been told that tomorrow your staff must work late because another department dropped the ball. You say:

❑ A.   Nothing, until tomorrow afternoon.

❑ B.   You ask for a show of hands of those who will be going home on time tomorrow. Then say: put your hands down.

❑ C.   It isn't my fault.

❑ D.   This is not my favorite kind of news. A client is in need and for us to deliver on time we will all need to work late tomorrow. I will try to find out what is being done to improve the process so this will not keep happening. Do you have any suggestions?

Scoring:  If you found none of the *Tacky Manager's* responses, you might want to spend some time reading from the suggested reading list or spend time with a therapist. Above all, do not talk to your employees.

If you found all thirty of the *Tacky Manager's* responses, you know *tacky* when you see it!

---

### WOULD YOU BELIEVE?

After reading a draft manuscript of *The Tacky Manager*, a tacky manager friend commented, "Is a good relationship with my support staff really *that* important?"

**It is *that* important if organizations want to improve!**

# A PERSONAL NOTE TO EMPLOYEES
# WHO READ THIS BOOK
# BEFORE GIVING IT TO THEIR TACKY MANAGERS

For the past twelve years I have conducted seminars and offered consultation on leadership development and related topics. I have heard every imaginable reason or excuse that keeps employees from doing their best.

We do not have to choose to be a victim to others' tackiness. Is is unfortunate that many give up because of their supervisors. They no longer seek the joy and pleasure that comes from doing work in a manner that affords joy and pleasure to others.

I wonder what would happen if words like...

**commitment,**

**creativity,**

**trust, and**

**team work**

...described our work environments?

Do you want to do something about it? If, in fact, we teach others how to treat us, we can retrain our tacky managers on what we are willing and not willing to tolerate. It is our choice to move from victim to **effective associate**. And, if by chance, you have seen yourself as *the tacky manager*, you can make choices today that will improve your effectiveness and make life better for your associates.

Would you like to contribute your *Tacky* story to the next edition of *The Tacky Manager* or to any of these books?

*The Tacky Professor*

*The Tacky Employee*

*The Tacky Doctor*

*The Tacky Attorney*

*The Tacky Teacher*

*The Tacky Principal*

*The Tacky Preacher*

Send **your** tacky anecdotes to:

> *THE TACKY MANAGER*
> P.O. BOX 431
> BRENTWOOD, TN  37024-0431

Order self adhesive decals, buttons, certificates for your manager, and some other *REALLY TACKY STUFF.* See order form on page 93.

## SUGGESTED RESOURCES

Belasco, James A., *Teaching The Elephant To Dance*

A practical, hands-on guide for creating the right kind of change in any organization. Belasco says that you can inspire and empower employees with a shared vision. Helpful to managers who are planning and implementing change.

Bennis, Warren, *Why Leaders Can't Lead*

An explanation of problems which face leaders and provides practical ideas on how to deal with troublesome issues. Bennis says if we do not acknowledge that employees are our primary asset, not our primary liability, then all the jealously held perks, power, and prerogatives will eventually count for nothing, because our companies will be acquired, merged, or sunk.

Covey, Stephen R., *The 7 Habits Of Highly Effective People*

A step-by-step pathway for living with fairness, integrity, honesty, and human dignity - principles that give us the security to adapt to change.

Byham, William C., *Zapp! the Lightning of Empowerment*

A guide for supervisors and managers on how to create an empowered organization. Zapp! shows how you can build job satisfaction and self-esteem as you improve profitability, competitiveness and team effectiveness.

Craig, Floyd and Anne, Craig Communications, Inc.

The Craigs have forbidden the use of their name associated in any way with this book (Only kidding). Craig Communications, Inc. is a public relations and marketing firm in Nashville, Tennessee.

Fratesi, Phil and Curtis, Anthony, Adventureworks

Experience-based learning that uses a variety of exciting outdoor challenges to effect change and growth with teams and individuals. Activities are designed to increase levels of trust and cooperation, promote willingness to take risks and accept responsibility, enhance self-confidence, and improve communication skills.

Lill, David, *Selling: The Profession*

You don't have to be a sales manager to find this resource helpful. Chapters are designed to stand on their own, offering specific help with significant issues facing managers.

Levering, Robert, *A Great Place To Work*

A look at specific practices that have made for good morale and good business at the very best workplaces. Levering explains how attitudes can affect success and points out the essential elements of a good workplace.

Gitlow, Howard and Shelly, *The Deming Guide To Quality and Competitive Position*

A practical treatment of Dr. W. Edwards Deming's 14 points. It offers a how-to guide for improving quality, productivity, and competitive position. The Gitlows say that managers must own up to their responsibility and must realize that the systems that they created and perpetuate cause approximately 85 percent of the problems.

Halbert, John E., *The Tacky Manager*

Must reading for you and your manager.

Jones, Doug, Doug Jones and Associates

Jones is a professional speaker and consultant based in Atlanta, Georgia. He is a master trainer in areas of sales, management, and productivity. His high energy presentations can help your organization turn ideas into action.

Scholtes, Peter R., *The Team Handbook*

There are many dimensions to Quality Leadership and project teams are one of the most important. Project teams stand a better chance of having significant impact on an organization's health than individual efforts because they represent the collective experience and knowledge of many people. The emphasis is on "how to" do the many things associated with teams: how to choose an appropriate mission, how to select the participants, how to run the team, how to create a plan for improvement, how to build teamwork.

Senge, Peter M., *The Fifth Discipline*

A guide to systems thinking and team learning. Senge identifies and discusses common learning disabilities in organizations and shows ways to overcome them. He says that "while traditional organizations require management systems that control people's behavior, learning organizations invest in improving the quality of thinking, the capacity for reflection and team learning, and the ability to develop shared visions...." His experience is that 90 percent of the time, what passes for commitment on the part of employees is actually compliance.

Walton, Mary, *The Deming Management Method*

Dr. Deming's management techniques are all carefully explained. It includes a step-by-step treatment of his major points and of their practical application. She quotes Dr. Deming: "Most so-called *goofing off* - [when] somebody seems to be lazy, doesn't seem to care - that person is almost always in the wrong job, or has **very poor management.**"

Other excellent resources:

Positive Employee Practices Institute - 1-800-476-8138

PEPI offers in-house training, consultation, a newsletter, and an annual conference. It showcases organizations whose people programs have made them highly successful and extraordinarily productive. PEPI believes that success depends on managers' abilities to develop and sustain an empowered work force.

Lakewood Publications - 50 South Ninth Street Minneapolis, MN 55402

Publisher of magazines, business newsletters, major national human resource conferences, and management resources catalogues. Lakewood Publications is on the leading edge of service quality and total quality research.

## ABOUT THE AUTHOR

John E. Halbert — consultant, teacher, businessman, speaker
par excellence — is known throughout the country for his
inspiring and information packed programs in the areas of
leadership development, customer service and total quality
management.

For more than ten years John has managed his own
consulting firm, IMPACT SEMINARS, INC., in Brentwood,
Tennessee. He brings a wealth of experience to his
company's clients and has received impressive accolades that
reflect his skills. As a contract presenter for an international
public seminar company, he received the Award for
Excellence and the top rating among eighty national speakers
at an International Customer Service Association
Conference.

Bringing superb organization and meticulously tailored
topical matter to his presentations, John captivates audiences
with his unique style. He makes training sessions not only
enjoyable, but extraordinarily successful from the standpoint
of both the audience and the organization by his skillful
blending of wit and practical information.

John's business experiences vary greatly. He has held
positions as director of human resource development for a
three hospital medical system and a major publishing house,
director of a not-for-profit social services agency, and a
founder and officer of a credit card company.

His wide speaking and consulting obligations have included
assignments in Europe and the Orient. In addition to the
*Tacky Manager,* John has written a book for children, *I Could
If I Wanted To.*

## ORDER FORM

| Quantity | Item | Price | Total |
|----------|------|-------|-------|
|  | *The Tacky Manager* | $9.95 | $ |
|  | Certificate | $2.00 | $ |
|  | Button | $3.00 | $ |

**TOTAL: $**_____

Price includes shipping and handling.
Tennessee residents add 77 cents per book sales tax.

❑ I have included a Tacky anedcdote on the reverse side of this form which can be used in subsequent printings which enables me to deduct $1.00 from this order.

Call for discount on quantities of 12 or more books.

❑ I am interested in Tacky Manager self adhesive decals featuring the illustrations from the book for use on mugs, trash baskets, my manager's door etc. Please send me an order form with prices on the following decal illustrations found on:

❑ Page 10  ❑ Page 12  ❑ Page 16  ❑ Page 18  ❑ Page 20
❑ Page 22  ❑ Page 30  ❑ Page 38  ❑ Page 40  ❑ Page 59
❑ Page 60  ❑ Page 66  ❑ Page 69  ❑ Other page ____

Ship to:

Name _____

Title _____

Organization _____

Address _____

City_____State_____Zip_____

❑ Visa  ❑ Mastercard #_____Exp. Date _____

Phone_____Signature _____

❑ check enclosed

**Mail order form to:**
*The Tacky Manager*
**P.O. Box 431**
**Brentwood, TN 37024-0431**

**Or fax order form to:**
**(615)-373-0958**